Prison Poems

by Bill Sheldon

2018

Berlin Federal Prison

Whilst in the slammer with nothing to do
I wrote a few poems I'll now share with you

Copyright ©2025 *Bill Sheldon*

All Rights Reserved

CONTENTS

THE HOLE 1

MY PLAN 2

EEL WGN 4

CAMPING 5

MEMORIES FROM BERLIN 7

TAXES 9

MY GOAL 10

THE FUTURE 11

SUNSHINE 14

SEE MORE 15

KEN IN THE PEN 17

GOODBYE BERLIN 19

BERLIN BILL 20

THE HOLE

I'm 71 and lived my life free from crime, I never did think I'd be doing jail time,
Then along came a warden with eels to sell, and tragically into his trap I soon fell.
He had a license, and I reported the sale, but as a result I wound up in jail.
He lied when he told me where he had caught um, I had lots of cash, so I gladly bought um.

I had broken the law, as a matter of fact, an old-timey law called the old Lacey Act,
It was a felony, with an awful big fine, and up to five years of hard prison time.
I went to court, and for mercy I pled, thank goodness the judge, he had a good head,
He fined me ten grand and confiscated my truck, to most people this would seem like bad luck.

He also said, "Billy you must go to jail," I said, "Thanks your honor, do I have any bail?"
He said, "Oh no Billy, I trust you my friend, just report to the prison camp up in Berlin."
I asked him, "How long must I go there to stay?" he answered, "Six months, right to the day."
I came here in June and will be out in December, and as it turns out, it's a good time to remember.

I've met some new friends and read lots of books, and by walking the track, I've changed my good looks.
I used to smoke weed and drank liquor too, and now that I'm clean, I feel pure and true.
There's Lefty and Shifty, Jesus and Jake, Stinky and Fatty, and one called the Snake.
I've dropped forty pounds and eat healthy now, when I came in here, I looked like a cow.

I'll soon be set free and be fishing again, making more money than I did in the pen.
I've got lots of cash, so I'll buy a new truck, and buy lots of eels with any kind of good luck.
My wife and my family are waiting for me, we'll go south this winter and live wild and free,
And when springtime comes and with it the eels, I'll be back in Maine, oh how good it feels.

I'll be making more money than I have a need for, but I'll save it in case that I ever am poor.
And if that day comes, and I need some cash, I'll go dig up my "HOLE" and get into my Stash.

MY PLAN

To get from here, to over there, most people ride in a car
They don't walk, like they used to do, they all say it's too far
So I've decided for the next whole year, I am a gonna walk
Whether it's to the grocery store, or just down to my dock

I don't think it'll be a problem, everything will be just fine
If I wanna go from A to B, It'll just take a little more time
I can't think of one good reason, not to always walk
There's plenty of roads, I've got good shoes, and to no one I'll have to talk

And while on my way, to wherever I'm going, there's lots for me to see
There'll be birds and squirrels, cats and dogs, and an occasional Bumble Bee
I'll walk from my home to my eel-buying shop, it's only 100 miles
It'll only take about a week, and in a backpack, I'll carry my files

I'll spend 11 weeks buying glass eels, and fishing for them too
At season's end, I'll walk back home, it'll be something new
Instead of late winter, it will then be spring, and it will probably rain
But I don't care, I like to get wet, and certainly won't cause me no pain

And when I get home, my legs will be strong, and in good health I will be
I'll have made lots of money, and had a good time, and surely I'll feel free
After I'm home, if my wife wants to go to a restaurant for a bite to eat
She can drive, but I will walk, why not, I've got two good feet

I think this is a good idea, and things will be just fine
No matter where I want to go, I'll just have to budget my time
To some people, this would not work well, and they would not have fun
But I like to walk, and if I am late, I'll change my gait to a run

I can dress warm when it's cold outside, and wear less if the temperature's hot
And if I feel good, instead of walking, I'll just break into a trot
I'll carry a Knap Sack on my back, if I'm going to the store
And I'll only buy just what I need, and not a single item more

Now, if my wife wants to take a vacation, and we have to take a plane
She can drive to the airport, but I'll walk there just the same
And when we get to where we're going, there'll probably be lots of sun
She can walk with me, it'll do her good, and together we'll have lots of fun

We'll go to the movies, or go to a play, or go to the beach to swim
And when we are done, we'll walk back to our room, both feeling fit and trim
And while we are there, if she should get, what they call the shopping bug
She can buy whatever she wants, but only what she can lug

I won't have to buy any truck insurance or spend any money on gas
And if I get tired while walking, I'll simply sit on my ass
I might take a nap in the shade of a tree
Or walk into the woods if I have to pee

And while walking along, whenever I feel, like I have got to shit
I'll use my foot, and dig a small hole, and squat right over it
I don't plan on using no paper, with which to wipe me ass
I'll use some leaves, or a smooth stick, or even a handful of grass

I'll have lots of time to think about life,
And how lucky I am to have such a nice wife
And when I decide to go out on my boat, I'll hoist up a great big sail,
And spend the day thinking how happy I am, not to still be in jail

EEL WGN

Seven before seven, ten before ten, on weekends, it's ten with no rest till the end.
This refers to the miles that I walk every day, it helps pass the time, while it's here I must stay.
Sentenced to prison for buying some eels, besides going to jail, they confiscated my wheels,
A Ford F-450 with dual tires on back, I bought it brand new, and the color was black.

I was proud of this truck and bought it with cash, it was all legal money and part of my stash.
I guess it was my way of kinda like braggin, with Maine license plates that said the "Eel Wgn"
There were two tanks in the back, all hooked up with air, and when I drove by, most people would stare.
The truck was complete with my name on the door, flood lights in the back, and four on the floor.

It costs me $500,000.00 to fill my tanks up with eels, this gives one great pleasure, and I know how that feels,
Cause when I unload them and sell them to Mitch, I know that I'm soon going to be very rich.
I bought them with cash and got cash in return, before I am done, I'll have money to burn.
But I will not burn it, I'll save it instead, and my heirs can have it, when I am dead.

The first thing I'll do when I get out of jail, is buy a new truck when I find one for sale,
It will be black, and it will be nice, and the tanks will be filled with cold water and ice.
My name and my logo will be on the door, and she'll carry glass eels to the market once more
As she rolls down the road with the back of it saggin, once again they will say, "There goes the Eel Wgn"

CAMPING

There are lots of guys here at the camp in Berlin, some are quite fat, while others quite thin
There's Fat Girl, and Mouth, and one they call Cookie, there's Brazil and Turkey and one who's a Bookie
There's Bullwinkle and Neat, and then there's Big D, there's Warren and Matty and the Kingpin, that's me
There's Julian and Ford and old "Tits Magee", and most of them feel that they should be free

Some are here for many years, but still they think of home, and all the things they'd like to do
And where they'd like to roam
Some are here for only months, and then they are set free, they're all called short-timers, and
This group includes me

Everyone has a story to tell, how the system was unjust,
Some were caught red-handed, but most in some big bust,
Some faced a jury, some only a judge, on account of an offered plea deal
But if they are here, they were found guilty, confirmed by official state seal

But time passes by, and all seem to adapt, and know that there'll come a day
When no longer jail time, for the crime they committed, is the price that they have to pay
And when they're set free, most have a plan, to never again return,
Some soon will slip up, and go back to court, and their fate, there they will soon learn

They're cuffed and they're shackled and put on a bus, and travel through several states
They're tired and hungry when they get here, and gawked at by all the inmates
Some meet old friends that served time together in some other far-away jail
And some of them realize it was a mistake when they simply chose to jump bail

They're given some clothes, and something to eat, and then they are led to a bed
It's very clear, they wish they weren't here, doesn't even need to be said
But soon, other inmates gather around them and offer them toothpaste and soap
Whatever they need is theirs for the asking, that is, everything but some dope

And in a week's time, they'll be standing in line, holding a bag in their hand
Which they will fill up, some to the top, in fact, all that the bag can stand
Cookies and crackers and all kinds of snacks, soups and stamps, coffee and macks
They'll all walk away with smiles on their faces and their bags slung over their backs

Two times a day, a count is conducted, and all must stand by their beds
So the guards can walk up and down the aisles, and count all the sad-looking heads
Sometimes, they get mad and they launch a search, usually wearing a frown
When they find a phone or maybe some smokes, they call for a total lockdown

They keep us inside without any TV, and nothing to do but read
There's no going to work, or commissary to get what we all want and need
It could last a week, or a very long time
Depending on how much they were able to find

Then, all of a sudden, they'll tell us someday
The lockdown is over, and we can go out and play
We can walk on the track, or play basketball
Or just sit in the sunshine, enjoying the fall

And now that they've quit being so mean
We can all get back to our daily routine
We can all have visits and watch TV again
Here at the prison camp in the town of Berlin

MEMORIES FROM BERLIN

I've got lots of memories from my stay here at Berlin,
The first day was the hardest for my sentence to begin,
So I asked Deb to help me, make it through until the end,
I don't know how she did it, but she sure did my friend

I was greeted with a shout, of "Here comes the Eel Kingpin,"
He had read about me in newspapers sent to him
All the bottom bunks were taken, so I got one on the top,
Till an inmate shouted, "That's no place to put the old man Pop'

So the guy that was on the bottom said, "I'll switch with you old man"
So I flopped down on the bottom bunk, my prison clothes in hand
Then someone gave me a toothbrush, another gave me some soap
The overwhelming kindness from the inmates gave me hope

The next morning, I went outside, that's when I spied the track
And there were mountains all around me to my front and to my back
Round and round I walked that day, thinking of my plight
And found it quite relaxing, and made it easy to sleep that night

I soon found out I had to work, down at the plant of power
It was not hard, but the pay sure sucked, at only twelve cents an hour
I never was much for reading books until I went to jail
Or writing letters to my friends, I always used e-mail

I spent my time writing, and I read fifty books,
And by walking the track I've changed my good looks
I lost fifty pounds during my stay at Berlin
Just from walking the track, and now I am thin

I got here in June and the weather was hot,
By the end of October, it had snowed quite a lot
And in wintertime, there's lots of wind and it's cold,
And the sky's full of clouds is what I've been told

Sean Herrman's been here many years, and knows what you can and cannot do
He passed this info on to me, so I wouldn't wind up in the SHU
Make sure you're standing by your bunk, when they count all of the men
That's the first rule that you learn, when you arrive here at Berlin

Keep away from contraband, and don't give the guards no sass
Many of the inmates snore and all of them's got gas
Don't ask any questions and do what you're told to do
Don't look with lust at the female guards or you'll be in the SHU

My brother dropped me off here, and he's coming to pick me up
I'll be so glad to see him in his big gray pick-up truck
When he dropped me off here, I was filled with fear
And now it's only a matter of hours, and I'll be outta here

The time has come for me to leave, and go back to my wife
Go back to catching baby eels, and live a normal life
There's one thing that I know for sure, bout the jail here in Berlin
I'll do my very best, n'err to come back here again

TAXES

It all started in twenty ten, two hundred a pound was the price back then,
Cash was paid for healthy eels, the buyers bought from trucks on wheels
The next year, the price climbed steady, and the fishers made sure that they were ready
To catch the eels as they came in, to miss a night was considered a sin

The price climbed up to one thousand per pound, the huge catch of eels was the talk of the town
All were happy, none were sad. It was the best year we ever had
In twenty twelve, the winter was mild, the eels were early, and the men went wild
Two thousand six hundred was now the price, the eels were thick and there was no ice

Several fishermen made a hundred grand, wading around in the rocks and sand
Some of the boys that had good gear, and knew just where to set
Saw thousands of eels swim up the river, go right into their net

The buyers gave them stacks of cash, and in return got eels
Some built homes some got boobs, and most got brand-new wheels
The Feds stepped in to get their share, but few had paid their taxes
It was a mess when the IRS jumped in and raised their axes

It soon became a real sad tale, and several fishermen went to jail
So the state stepped in and changed the law,
Cash could no longer be paid for eels, and checks are what we saw
They also told the buyers they had to have a shop,
Buying riverside out of trucks simply had to stop

Each man that wanted to sell some eels, had to have a card
The state knew just what each man caught, and poaching is quite hard
Quotas were established on how many could be caught
And the state knew just how many eels, every buyer bought
And now the fishery runs quite smooth, and big money is still made,
But now instead of hiding it, the taxes must be paid.

MY GOAL

Four thousand laps around the track is what I've walked so far,
The surface of the track's quite hard, cause it's made out of tar
I've had blisters on my heels and toes, competing for the pain
I never let that bother me, I kept walking just the same

Through wind and rain and scorching heat, and even sometimes cold
I walked just like an athlete who was chasing after gold
But gold was not what I was seeking, weight loss was my game
I was fat when I began, now skinny Bill's my name

The first four hundred miles I walked, my knee gave me great pain
I had decided if it got worse, that I would use a cane
But soon, it seemed to disappear, and my blisters were all gone
I never was so happy and I never felt so strong

I soon decided to set a goal, to walk one thousand miles,
I wasn't going to sit around all day, and maybe get the Piles
So round and round the track I walked, ten miles or more each day
Feeling good but tired was the only price I had to pay

I've lost fifty pounds and I look a whole lot smaller
I'm a whole lot thinner, but I'm surely no taller
I came to Jail on the seventh of June,
And like a guitar, I got my body in tune

I'm still in jail, but I feel good, about the path I chose,
The only thing that I need now, are some brand new clothes
My wife will buy them for me, and send them in the mail,
So I'll have some clothes that fit me, when they let me out of jail

The only thing that I need now, are some brand new clothes

THE FUTURE

Sean Herrman is a good friend of mine,
Up in Berlin, he's still doing time
The judge sent him up for selling much weed
Lots of mates smoke it, he was just filling their need

Sean hails from cape cod, way down in Mass.
Sean and his family all like to smoke grass
Now the cops they were looking to fill up this new jail
And soon they were on poor old Sean's tail

They got him in twelve and sent him to jail
He n'err had a chance to even post bail
But Sean is no dummy, and makes the best of his time
He reads lots of books, and is doing just fine

He helps other inmates when they arrive at this jail
As much as a schooner is helped by a sail
He gives them advice, and shows them the way
To stay out of trouble day after day

Sean's the biggest man at the camp where I'm at
Not only in stature, but what's under his hat
He proves this each day with cunning finesse
While he's debating or just playing chess

He's a lot smarter than the average caveman
And when he gets out, he's got a good plan
To get a smart woman, to help him through life
Cause he'll know how to act, round his soon-to-be wife

He grasps this new movement, they call it "me too"
That tells you just what, you can, and can't do
He'll know how to please her, and he'll call her honey
And knowing Big Sean, she'll have lots of money

He won't have to work, and he'll spend his time fishing
He'll bring his wife with him, just like he's been wishing
For all of these years while sitting in jail
To open his beers and fetch his lunch pail

She'll wear a bikini, that she will fill out
And they'll have a big boat, on this, there's no doubt
And when fishing's slow, and there's no more to be said
He'll take her below deck and get her in bed

And when they come home and tie up the boat
In front of their house, that has a big float
He'll cook her some supper, and serve her some wine
Cause he learned how to cook while serving his time

He'll wash up the dishes, and then do the floor
And ask her if she would like to have more
And if she says no, he'll go fill up the tub
And ask her if she would like a back rub

And when she's all done and ready for bed
He'll fluff up the pillow for her beautiful head
And if she wants to have sex, he'll give her that too
He knows how to treat women, and knows just what to do

And when they're all done and she falls asleep
Back down the stairs, old Sean will soon creep
He'll reach in his pocket, and pull out his bag
And roll up a fatty with one orange zig zag

He'll go to the fridge, and grab a cold beer

Then plop down on the couch, and pull the ashtray up near

And when he's all done and he's caught a good buzz

He'll think about prison, and how bad it was

SUNSHINE

I came to Berlin on the sixth day of June, I felt terrible, like a guitar out of tune
The longer I'm here, the more I can see, that even a prison camp is no place for me
Most of the guards are real Pecker Heads, The bunks that we sleep in are not like real beds
The floor is cement, as cold as can be, The windows don't open, this is no place for me

The inmates are noisy and up half the night, talking on cellphones, some high as a kyte
Others are snoring, and some of them farting, I can't wait for the day that I'll be departing
The leaves have all turned and in full color bold, temperature's dropping and it's getting cold
Summer is gone and winter is near, November is coming and I can leave here

And one thing I know as sure as there's sin, I'll never come back to this camp in Berlin
I'll catch lots of eels, and make lots of money, and the rest of my days will be bright and sunny

SEE MORE

Last night I went to sleep and I had a funny dream,
It was the funniest thing that I have ever seen,
A bow-legged guard, waddling along
Walking like he might be wearing a thong

He acted tough, but what a farce
If he picked up much weight, he'd fall on his arse
His hair was grey and his vision was poor
He was wearing glasses so he could "SEE MORE"

His pants were baggy, but his shirt was tight
Now I'm telling you, he was quite a sight
His legs were short, but his arms were long
He sure looks funny, walking along

But he was a guard with plenty of power,
To make you work for just twelve cents an hour
And when I told him I was all done at the plant
"I won't allow you to quit," he said "You just can't"

We need your slave labor to keep the shithouses clean
I can't make the guards do it, that would be mean
That is a job that the prisoners must do
Drug dealers and users and people like you

So I asked him, "How long must I work here for you?"
"I'm an old man and my back hurts me too"
He said he don't care, and he'd let me know
Now go back to work and shovel some snow

So I said, "Ok sir you are the boss"
Did your legs get bowed out like that from riding a hoss?
He said do you know what I'm gonna do?
For that little comment you go to the SHU.

So I said thanks, fatso, you're quite a jerk
I got what I wanted, now I don't have to work
And whilst in the SHU, I'll think about eels
And making some money, oh how good it feels.

KEN IN THE PEN

There are 75 guys at the prison camp in Berlin,
Most seem at home here, except one they call Ken
Ken rides a Harley, and he likes to hunt,
And if there was trouble, I'd want him up front

He's the kind of a guy you don't give no sass
Cause if you're not careful, you'll be on your ass
He lifts weights each day and he walks on the track
And if you are his friend, he'll cover your back

He works at the camp welding five days a week
Repairing broken backhoes and pipes that do leak
He built a big moose all made out of steel
And one thing for certain, it sure does look real

Now one thing that's true, as sure as there's sin
He loves his wife, and she sure loves him
She shows this by coming here weekends without fail
To see her Ken Bailey, even though he's in jail

He also has friends that ride their bikes here,
They've got lots of tattoos, and they like to drink beer
And when he gets out, if he needs a hand
They can be counted on, man for man

Ken's a straight shooter, and he's not a drugger,
He's only in here cause he helped some poor bugger
And in return for his help, the guy ratted him out
To save his own ass, on this, there's no doubt

Ken went to court, and for mercy, he pled,

The judge showed no mercy and gave him two years instead

But he'll soon be set free and be home with his wife

Anxious and ready to start a new life

Ken's favorite pastime is stalking big Bucks,

Catching big fish, and driving old trucks

Because he's a felon, he can't have a gun

But this will not stop him from having his fun

He'll switch to his Bow or his old flintlock gun,

And go hunting once more with ole Hoss, his big son

They'll leave before sunup, and NOT count on luck

To come back to the camp, with a big buck in the truck

GOODBYE BERLIN

Many people wind up in jail, because they were caught stealing,
I wound up in the slammer, because I was caught glass eeling,
So here I am in old Berlin, never thought I'd be in the pen
All the inmates dress in brown, the guards all dress in blue
The one place you don't want to go, is the place they call the SHU

Some are here for many years, for selling coke and weed,
It was the only way they had, to get just what they need
They did it for the money, there's no disputing that,
Everything was going fine, until they sold some to a rat

It is no fun to be locked up, and told just what to do,
The food's no good, the beds are hard, it makes one feel quite blue
But time goes by, and plans are made, and soon you are set free
It's a happy day for all concerned, on this we can agree

I miss my home and my dog, but most of all my wife,
I can not wait to get out of here, and start a brand-new life
And there's one thing that I'm sure of, just you wait and see,
The Berlin Federal Prison Camp will n'err again see me

Bill Sheldon, 2018
Berlin Federal Prison Camp

BERLIN BILL

It was Northern New Hampshire, up Berlin way,
Where I'd met a new inmate, who'd stopped in for a stay
Judge Levy had sentenced him to six months in the clink
Six months with no reefer, no booty, no drink

In here, he met Seymor, a cop from Kentucky
Who should have been stillborn, but somehow got lucky
Seymor said, "Bill it's my world, and now you are in it"
"You'll work every day, up to the last minute"

What he didn't know, but he would soon learn,
Was that old Bill Sheldon had energy to burn
Bill spent his time out walking the track
He walked 1300 miles, and never looked back

Because you can't keep a man like Bill Sheldon down
He rolls out of his bunk wearing a smile, not a frown
He's a self-made man, forged by hard work
He don't need the opinion of some Kentucky jerk

Bill was polite but had plenty of Pluck,
Like the time he told Herrman, shut up you fat fuck
Bill leaves in the morning, back to the grind
He can't wait to get home, relax, and unwind
He won't miss the bullshit, the troubles, the drama
He just wants to get home and cuddle with Mama

But he better get rested, and enjoy being free
Cause his fortune is breeding in the Sargasso Sea
Soon there'll be eels, coming by the billions
These glass eels are how old Bill made his millions

I'm going to miss him, on this, there's no doubt

I hope that I see him, when I'm finally out

I think that I'll call him in twenty twenty-five

Till then, I'll be called inmate one twenty-nine fifty-five

Good luck Bill, it's been a pleasure doing time with you.

I spent the next 15 years in the lobster industry where I applied for and was granted two United States Patents, one titled " A System For Transporting Lobsters And Other Marine Organisms In Aerated Sea Water," the other one is an"Underwater Vacuum For Harvesting Lobsters And Other Marine Species."

In the early nineties the demand and the price for elvers increased, I began fishing for, buying, and exporting them to markets overseas.

In South Carolina, in 2011, I bought some elvers that I knew had been harvested illegally. The rat that sold them to me was an undercover warden, wearing a mic, he had a valid elver harvesting license, and I reported the transaction to S.C. Fisheries Department, as required. However , since I knew he caught them illegally (he told me),

when I crossed the state line with them I was arrested, charged and convicted of violating an 1800's law called the Lacy Act. I was fined $10,000.00, they confiscated my $80,000.00 Eel Wgn , and put me in federal Prison for six months.

The poems in this book "Prison Poems " are about how I wound up in prison, what I did whilst serving my time there, and some of the interesting characters that I met

BILL SHELDON

50 Premium Mustard Dishes

By: Kelly Johnson